THE EXPANDING UNITED STATES

The Rise of Nationalism 1812-1820

TITLE LIST

THE EXPANDING UNITED STATES
The Rise of Nationalism 1812-1820

BY

ELLYN SANNA

MASON CREST PUBLISHERS
PHILADELPHIA

THE EXPANDING UNITED STATES

Mason Crest Publishers Inc.
370 Reed Road
Broomall, Pennsylvania 19008
(866) MCP-BOOK (toll free)

First printing
1 2 3 4 5 6 7 8 9 10

Library of Congress Cataloging-in-Publication Data

Sanna, Ellyn, 1958-
 The expanding United States : The rise of nationalism (1812/1820) / by Ellyn Sanna.
     p. cm. — (How America became America)
 Includes bibliographical references and index.
 ISBN 1-59084-905-1 ISBN 1-59084-900-0 (series)
 1. United States—Politics and government—1809-1817—Juvenile literature. 2. United States—Politics and government—1817-1825—Juvenile literature. 3. United States—Territorial expansion—Juvenile literature. 4. Nationalism—United States—History—19th century—Juvenile literature. I. Title. II. Series.
 E341.S26 2005
 973.5'1—dc22

                          2004029142

Design by Dianne Hodack.
Produced by Harding House Publishing Service, Inc.
Cover design by Dianne Hodack.
Printed in the Hashemite Kingdom of Jordan.

CONTENTS

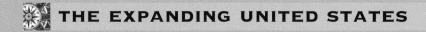

INTRODUCTION

by Dr. Jack Rakove

Today's America is not the same geographical shape as the first American colonies—and the concept of America has evolved as well over the years.

When the thirteen original states declared their independence from Great Britain, most Americans still lived within one or two hours modern driving time from the Atlantic coast. In other words, the Continental Congress that approved the Declaration of Independence on July 4, 1776, was continental in name only. Yet American leaders like George Washington, Benjamin Franklin, and Thomas Jefferson also believed that the new nation did have a continental destiny. They expected it to stretch at least as far west as the Mississippi River, and they imagined that it could extend even further. The framers of the Federal Constitution of 1787 provided that western territories would join the Union on equal terms with the original states. In 1803, President Jefferson brought that continental vision closer to reality by purchasing the vast Louisiana Territory from France. In the 1840s, negotiations with Britain and a war with Mexico brought the United States to the Pacific Ocean.

This expansion created great opportunities, but it also brought serious costs. As Americans surged westward, they created a new economy of family farms and large plantations. But between the Ohio River and the Gulf of Mexico, expansion also brought the continued growth of plantation slavery for millions of African Americans. Political struggle over the extension of slavery west of the Mississippi was one of the major causes of the Civil War that killed hundreds of thousands of

Americans in the 1860s but ended with the destruction of slavery. Creating opportunities for American farmers also meant displacing Native Americans from the lands their ancestors had occupied for centuries. The opening of the west encouraged massive immigration not only from Europe but also from Asia, as Chinese workers came to labor in the California Gold Rush and the building of the railroads.

By the end of the nineteenth century, Americans knew that their great age of territorial expansion was over. But immigration and the growth of modern industrial cities continued to change the American landscape. Now Americans moved back and forth across the continent in search of economic opportunities. African Americans left the South in massive numbers and settled in dense concentrations in the cities of the North. The United States remained a magnet for immigration, but new immigrants came increasingly from Mexico, Central America, and Asia.

Ever since the seventeenth century, expansion and migration across this vast landscape have shaped American history. These books are designed to explain how this process has worked. They tell the story of how modern America became the nation it is today.

One
THE GROWTH OF AMERICAN NATIONALISM

The word "nationalism" would have made no sense to someone born in medieval England or in North America before the Europeans' arrival. These individuals drew their sense of identity from the small groups to which they belonged; in the case of medieval England, ordinary people were tied to the land and gave service to the nobility who ruled them directly, while native North Americans identified themselves by the tribal group to which they belonged. Neither group would have thought to connect their identity with a large ruling government, nor a widespread geographical area.

But at the close of the Middle Ages, a new concept arose in Europe: the nation, a centralized and powerful government that controlled a large geographical region. The great European nations took shape over the following centuries—England, Spain, Germany, Italy, and France being some of the most important—and the inhabitants of these nations felt a gradually growing sense of pride in the nation to which they belonged. These larger populations were further linked by shared cultural customs, language, and religion. They also felt a sense of competition with the other lands around them. Just as sports teams vie for supremacy, so did nations, but "winning" at the national level was measured by power, land, wealth—and all too often, in human lives.

When the United States was born from the thirteen original English colonies, at first Americans were linked mainly by their desire for political independence. Even in the midst of the Revolutionary War, many of the "rebels"

Map of North America in 1811

The Rise of Nations

Many historians feel that certain conditions are necessary for the growth of nations. One of the most important is a system of communication that can tie together a larger population. From this perspective, it is no accident that nations first arose in Europe in the years after the invention of the printing press.

still considered themselves English; they had not yet begun to think of themselves as members of a new nation.

But as the years went by, the United States' government grew and matured, and at the same time, its citizens began to identify themselves as "Americans." They were drawn together by their pride in the exciting story of their successful fight for independence; they shared a language, a common concept of God, and a growing belief in their right to the North American wilderness. They prided themselves on their courage in the face of danger, their hardiness in the midst of ongoing challenges, and

their willingness to work hard to protect and build their homes. As new generations were born, they no longer even considered thinking of themselves as English. They were Americans.

One of the necessary requirements for a nation is a sense of permanence. The nation's members need to know they are part of something lasting rather than a temporary arrangement. The Founding Fathers must have wondered if their great experiment in democracy would endure the test of time, but as the years went by, they and their children began to count on America's future. They were confident that their children, their grandchildren, their great

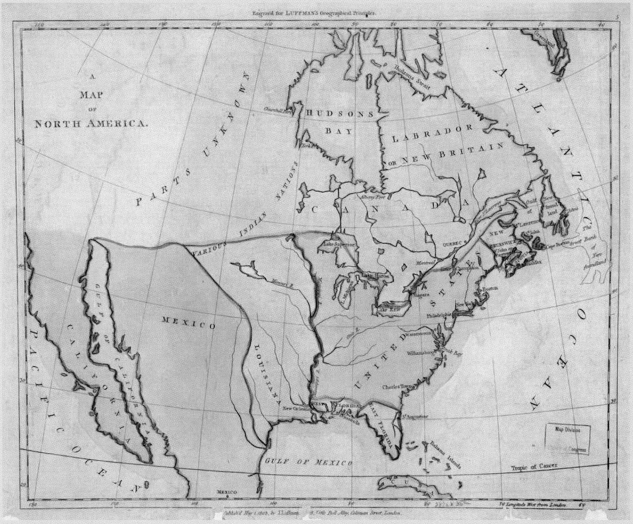

The United States in 1803

grandchildren, and all the generations that followed would also be Americans.

America's first president, George Washington, had warned his nation to stay out of foreign quarrels. But as Thomas Jefferson's presidency came to an end, he left America well on its way to war. The growing tension between the United States and the older nations of England and France may have helped build the young country's sense of itself as a nation in its own right; in the face of outside conflict, Americans drew together. And as nationalism grew to be a prevailing sentiment among Americans, it may in turn have done its part to heighten these same tensions.

Shortly after the American Revolution, France had undergone a revolution of its own. In many ways, it was a much messier sort of affair than America's, and the winners had a habit of chopping off the heads of those they had defeated or even of those who simply disagreed with the prevailing thought. Out of this upheaval, Napoleon Bonaparte emerged as France's leader, filled with nationalist fervor of his own. Determined to build France into an empire, the "Little Corporal," as Napoleon was called, set about conquering most of Europe. England's response was to declare war on France.

At first, Americans were determined to stay neutral in this European conflict. But neither England nor France looked on the baby nation of America as a power to be respected in its own right. Both nations captured American ships and sailors. English sea captains made the American sailors work on British ships (a practice referred to as impressment). Americans were understandably angry.

The fact that England seemed to feel entitled to the American **frontier** made Americans even angrier. After the Revolutionary

*A country's **frontier** is its unsettled land.*

Not Everyone Agrees

Not everyone agrees that nationalism is a good thing. *Antinationalism* is the idea that nationalism is a dangerous attitude that inevitably leads to conflict and war. According to this line of thought, nationalism builds walls between groups of human beings who might otherwise recognize that they have much in common; it emphasizes differences and encourages people to think of their own nation as better than all others, their citizens more valuable than other human beings, and their interests more pressing than anyone else's. Other philosophers, however, argue that we shouldn't confuse some of nationalism's potential negative consequences with the positive benefits of pride in one's country; in other words, we shouldn't throw out the baby with the bathwater!

Napoleon Bonaparte

*If something is **repealed**, it is officially abolished.*

__Neutrality__ is the state of not taking sides in a conflict.

War, England had formally granted the United States all its land on the North American continent—but despite this agreement, British troops had never left the forts England had built west of the Appalachian Mountains. The British seemed to assume that it was only a matter of time before the United States would be once more part of Britain's empire.

During Jefferson's presidency, he had tried to avoid war by taking economic measures to influence England. His Embargo Act, which prohibited all exports and nearly all imports, was meant to be a blow to both France's and England's economies.

The Global Movement

In today's world, *globalization* is a word with growing importance. The movement to form groups of continental or even worldwide organizations can be seen in the United Nations and the European Union, as well as economic alliances like the North American Free Trade Agreement (NAFTA). Globalization recognizes the need for all of Earth's inhabitants to work together to solve common challenges, such as those presented by environmental issues, the economy, and terrorism. The growth of the Internet and an international economy has meant that more and more people recognize that the Earth cannot be divided into separate, unconnected pieces. What affects one nation will sooner or later affect people even on the other side of the world.

At the beginning of the nineteenth century, this idea would have seemed as strange and nonsensical as nationalism would have seemed to both a North American Indian and a European in the years before the formation of the European nations.

Unfortunately, it was also a blow to America's economy. American farmers and merchants had depended on trade with foreign nations, and they were furious with Jefferson. Shortly before Jefferson left office, he reluctantly **repealed** the Embargo Act and replaced it with the Non-Intercourse Act, which allowed the United States to resume trade with all foreign nations except England and France.

James Madison, who followed Jefferson as president in 1810, had much in common with his predecessor, and he too wanted to avoid war. However, the Non-Intercourse Act proved to be impossible to enforce; rebellious American merchants simply refused to comply. In May of 1810, Congress passed Macon's Bill No. 2, which allowed trade with all nations. If, however, either France or England would agree to respect America's *neutrality* in their war, then the United States would no longer trade with the other nation.

Napoleon promptly promised he would respect American neutrality, and President Madison again halted all commerce with

Scene from colonial America

British impressment of U.S. soldiers

England. But many Americans were not satisfied. They wanted to prove to England once and for all that the United States was a nation in its own right, worthy of respect. America's honor was at stake—and they were eager to go to war to defend it.

Not all Americans agreed. Most New Englanders were against war because they depended on their sea trade with England. Older Americans like President Madison remembered the long and bloody years of the Revolutionary War, and they had no desire to plunge their land into another violent conflict.

But a new generation of hot-blooded leaders had risen up in the United States, men like Henry Clay and Andrew Jackson who came

James Madison

Henry Clay

from the South and the West, respectively, and these men pushed hard for war. They were eager to teach England a lesson, and they wanted to extend U.S. territory. The War Hawks, as they were called, finally convinced President Madison that war was his only option.

Ultimately, British impressments of American sailors had little to do with the War of 1812. On June 16, 1812, three days before America went to war with England, the British government promised to stop capturing American seamen. The United States went ahead and declared war anyway. The real cause of the war was not what was happening on the ocean but on land, along the western frontier.

In the western forts, the British troops had formed alliances with North American Indians. English soldiers helped the Indians protect their land from the encroaching American settlers. But American War Hawks were land hungry. They wanted the western Indian lands for themselves. They even cast greedy eyes at Canada to the north and Florida to the south. Filled with pride in their young nation and righteous anger against England, the War Hawks rushed gladly into battle with anyone who stood in their way—including the Native tribes.

Two
STRANGE ALLIES

On March 9, 1768, an enormous shooting star flamed across the night sky above the land we now know as Ohio. At the very instant the meteor lit the darkness, a Shawnee chief heard the cry of his newborn son. The chief knew it was a sign his son was destined for great things. He called the child Tekamthi, which meant "Panther Passing Across," for he believed the star was the spirit of a great panther passing over the Earth.

As Tekamthi grew up, he proved to be faster, more skillful, and more intelligent than all those around him. He made friends with a white boy and learned to speak, read, and write English—but he also learned the wisdom of his people: the ways of plants and animals, the ancient stories, and the power of the Great Spirit who ruled all life.

As Tekamthi grew older, he learned to respect some white men, while he hated others. White men killed his father; they took away his people's hunting land; and over and over, white men broke their promises. "We gave them forest-clad mountains, valleys full of game," he said. "In return they gave us . . . rum and trinkets and a grave."

Tekamthi wanted to make the white men leave his people in peace. If all the tribes united against their common enemy, Tekamthi believed they would have the strength to make the white men stay on the eastern side of the Appalachian Mountains. After all, Tekamthi said, a single strand of hair can be easily broken, but a braid is too strong to break. Tekamthi intended to braid his people together, creating a force too powerful for the white men to defeat. He still hoped to be able to find a peaceful solution to the conflict—but if the white men refused to cooperate, he was willing to fight.

*A **shaman** is a communicator between the physical and spiritual worlds, who is said to possess powers of healing and prophecy.*

*A **confederation** is a group of individual, independent organizations who join to cooperate for a common benefit.*

Tekamthi's brother, Tenskwatawa, was a ***shaman*** respected for his wisdom and spiritual power. The two brothers worked together to draw their people away from white men's ways, back to the strength they had once had. While Tenskwatawa led a spiritual revival, Tekamthi instigated a political movement.

Tekamthi recognized the threat the whites posed to all Native tribes, and he believed no treaty would ever protect the Indians for long against the white men's greed for land. The only way to combat this threat, Tekamthi believed, was for all the tribes to unite—not in a temporary ***confederation*** with each tribe keeping its own government (as had been tried before), but in a single political body with unified leadership. That way if the whites wanted to purchase land or draw up a treaty, they would not be able to play one tribe against the other as they had in the past; instead, they would have to deal with a unified government that represented the interests of all the tribes. And if the whites decided to go to war against

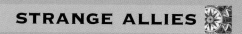

Tekamthi

the Native people, they would face an enormous army made up of warriors from all the tribes.

The brothers carried their message far and wide. They traveled east through the land known as New York, and then west past the Mississippi River and as far south as the Gulf of Mexico. Everywhere they went, they gathered followers, *plaiting* the people of many tribes into a strong braid. Soon, even the white settlers had heard of the two brothers' mission. Those who spoke English called the two brothers Tecumseh and the Prophet.

Some white Protestant ministers came to hear the brothers speak. Afterward, one of the ministers wrote:

The Prophet

> Our feelings were like Jacob's when he cried out "surely the Lord is in this place. . . ." Although these poor Shawnees have had no particular instruction but what they received from the outpouring of the Spirit, yet in point of real light and understanding, as well as behavior, they shame the Christian world.

Tekamthi (actual likeness)

But William Henry Harrison, the governor of the Indiana Territory, was not as favorably impressed with Tecumseh and the Prophet. More and more white settlers were moving into the territory, and Harrison worried that the Shawnee brothers would prove to be a danger to the settlers. In 1811, while Tecumseh was visiting the tribes in faraway Alabama, Harrison led his troops against the Shawnee camp on the Tippecanoe River, where the Prophet had been left in charge.

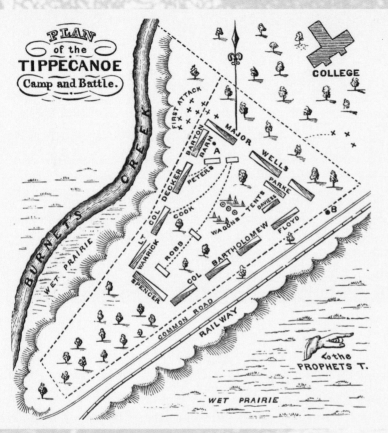

Map of Tippecanoe battle

Army trooper patrolling Indian territory

Plaiting *means weaving strands together to form a braid or rope.*

The Prophet put his confidence in the Great Spirit. He told the warriors that the Spirit would protect them, and the white men's bullets would merely bounce off their chests. This proved not to be the case.

Harrison destroyed the Shawnee village. His victory made him a national hero, and Americans gave him the nickname "Old

Wise Words from Tecumseh

"So live your life that the fear of death can never enter your heart. Trouble no one about their religion; respect others in their view, and demand that they respect yours. Love your life, perfect your life, beautify all things in your life. Seek to make your life long and its purpose in the service of your people. . . . Show respect to all people and grovel to none. When you arise in the morning give thanks for the food and for the joy of living. If you see no reason for giving thanks, the fault lies only in yourself. Abuse no one and no thing, for abuse turns the wise ones to fools and robs the spirit of its vision. When it comes your time to die, be not like those whose hearts are filled with the fear of death, so that when their time comes they weep and pray for a little more time to live their lives over again in a different way. Sing your death song and die like a hero going home."

William Henry Harrison

Tippecanoe." Meanwhile, the Shawnee lost their confidence in the Prophet's leadership. Tekamthi's strong braid was beginning to unravel.

But Tecumseh and the Prophet were not prepared to give up their quest. Tecumseh allied his forces with the British. The ancient nation from across the sea and the new and wobbly confederation of Native tribes may have seemed like strange partners, but they shared a common goal: hindering the growth of the young upstart, the United States.

Tecumseh

Harrison fighting the Shawnee

The End of the Story

Tecumseh died while fighting the troops led by William Henry Harrison in the War of 1812. Harrison, meanwhile, would become the United States' ninth president twenty-nine years later. White settlers soon settled the Indiana Territory, and treaty after treaty between the United States and the Native Americans was broken, just as Tecumseh had feared.

American Army and Navy during the War of 1812

Three
THE WAR OF 1812

The United States entered the War of 1812 in a rush of pride and spirit—and not much else. The country was deeply divided about the war. Many congressmen and senators had voted against it, and a large percentage of Americans did not want their country involved in a military conflict with England. America's armed forces were poorly prepared—and there were only 12,000 of them—and the U.S. Secretary of War William Eustis lacked military foresight. What's more, the troops were led mostly by officers who had achieved their rank through their political connections rather than by their military skills.

It was no wonder then that America's attacks on Canada were all abysmal failures. The War Hawks had assumed America could simply march into Canada and claim the land; Henry Clay had even boasted that the Kentucky *militia* could do the job all by itself. The three-pronged attack on Canada proved to be a total disappointment for the United States.

The U.S. military planners had decided to send three forces against the British in Canada: the first would move into Upper Canada through Detroit, Michigan; the second would cross the Niagara River; and the third would penetrate Montreal across

*A **militia** is a group of non-military citizens organized to perform military service.*

27

Pirate Jean Lafitte, Hero of the War of 1812

Pirate ship

Jean Lafitte hated being called a pirate; in his mind, he was a "privateer," someone who met an economic need in America. From the Gulf of Mexico through the waterways of Louisiana, he and his ships plundered the Caribbean Coast and the Atlantic—and then sold their cargo to those who lived in the Mississippi Delta. This region had become part of the United States as a result of the Louisiana Purchase of 1803. The French-speaking inhabitants seemed very different from the rest of America; besides, the U.S. government was too busy with international problems to pay much attention to this wild, remote region. America more or less abandoned the wetland with its foreign cultures to fend for itself. Lafitte sold his merchandise—fabrics, spices, trinkets, furniture, and utensils—at discount prices to the grateful residents. In short, he helped to feed and clothe a part of the new nation its government had overlooked. Although he wasn't exactly a Robin Hood who stole from the rich to give to the poor, the poor were nevertheless thankful for his services.

Lafitte never attacked an American ship. As a pirate, he was a "man without a country," but he admired the ideals expressed by the American constitution. When the new Louisiana governor arrested him, imprisoned him, and ruined his economic empire, Lafitte remained loyal to the United States. In the midst of the War of 1812, when America needed him most, Lafitte stepped forward to help fight the British.

The U.S.S. Constitution

Lake Champlain. Although the battle plan might have looked good on paper, it didn't work in practice. Instead, American forces not only failed to invade Canada, they also lost the city of Detroit. The militiamen who crossed the Niagara River were immediately pinned down and defeated. And the troops who were supposed to win Montreal mutinied and refused to fight at all.

Luckily for the United States, things went better for the American forces at sea. The British navy was famous for its power, and it

Misnamed

The War of 1812 might be better called the "War of 1812 to 1815," because that's how long the fighting lasted. Schoolchildren during the nineteenth century learned about the "Second Revolution," the war that firmly and forever established America's independence from England.

brought more than a thousand ships to blockade U.S. ports. Meanwhile, America had only fourteen seaworthy vessels to its name, plus a ragtag bunch of pirate ships willing to fight for the Americans. Amazingly, however, when the American ships had a chance to engage the British in one-on-one battles, they emerged victorious.

The most famous sea battle took place off the coast of Massachusetts between the British **frigate** *Guerriere* and the American U.S.S. *Constitution*. The British cannonballs literally bounced off the *Constitution*'s sides. "Huzza! Her sides are made of iron!" exclaimed one of the American sailors. The ship was actually made of wood covered with a thin layer of copper to

keep out worms—but the hull was more than two feet thick, made of the hardest wood in the world (live oak, which grows in the American South). After the *Constitution* emerged victorious from her battle with the *Guerriere*, Americans called her "Old Ironsides," and she became a symbol of American pride and hope.

Despite the individual successes of the *Constitution* and other American ships, however, the British navy was able to wrap a stranglehold around U.S. ports. Unable to ship goods in and out of the country, American merchants and farmers suffered, and the U.S. economy faltered nearly to a standstill.

But America did not give up. New attempts to invade Canada were still not successful, but

Old Ironsides

*A **frigate** is a fast, medium-sized, square-rigged fighting ship used in the 18th and 19th centuries.*

The U.S.S. Constitution

Oliver Hazard Perry

The *Constitution*'s career as a warship lasted eighty-four years. During that time, she survived forty-two battles and was never defeated; the only enemy ever aboard her were prisoners. The ship inspired Oliver Wendell Holmes' poem "Old Ironsides." Today, the *Constitution* is a museum ship docked in Boston's harbor; nearly a million people visit her each year.

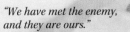

*"We have met the enemy,
and they are ours."*

32

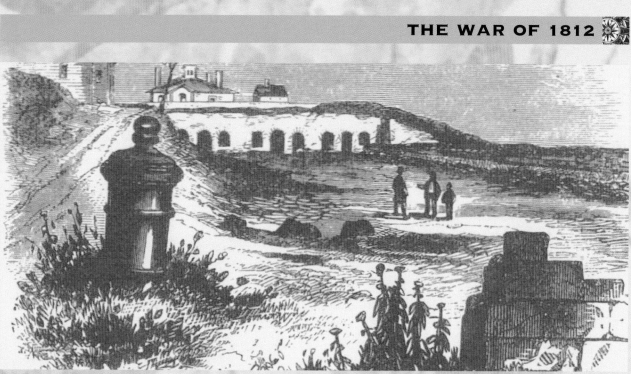

Fort Sewall, near Marblehead, Massachusetts, scene of War of 1812 action

American general William Henry Harrison (the same man who proved to be Tecumseh's downfall) was building his troops' strength in the West. By the summer of 1813, he had put together an army of 8,000 men.

Meanwhile, a young navy officer named Oliver Hazard Perry had built an inland navy to sail the Great Lakes. His first battle against the British on Lake Erie destroyed the entire enemy squadron. Afterward, he sent a message to General Harrison that would live forever in history: "We have met the enemy, and they are ours."

Perry's triumph meant that the British troops in the West were now cut off from their supply lines. The British abandoned Fort Malden and began retreating eastward, away from Detroit. Harrison overtook them and de-

Letter from First Lady Dolley Madison to Her Sister (August 23–24, 1814)

"Will you believe it, my sister? We have had a battle, or skirmish . . . and here I am still, within sound of the cannon! Mr. Madison comes not. May God protect us! . . . At this late hour a wagon has been procured, and I have filled it with plate and the most valuable articles, belonging to the house. . . . I insist on waiting until the large picture of George Washington is secured and it requires to be un-screwed from the wall. This process was found too tedious for these perilous moments; I have or-dered the frame to be broken, and the canvas taken out. It is done!"

Seceding *means leaving an organization or government.*

feated them at the Battle of the Thames. (This was the battle where Tecumseh died.) Things were starting to look up for the Americans.

But right about then, England finally defeated Napoleon—which meant the British could now turn their full attention to the war in America. More ships and more troops sailed across the Atlantic, ready to attack the unruly Americans with renewed vigor.

Dolley Madison

The British planned to attack the United States on three fronts: New York, along Lake Champlain and the Hudson River, severing New England from the rest of the country; New Orleans, blocking the Mississippi River, on which so much American trade and transportation depended; and the Chesapeake Bay, a diversionary tactic intended to draw the U.S. forces away from the other two targets. The British wanted to bring America to its knees, hoping that in the end, the United States would give up much of its territory to England.

By the fall of 1814, things were looking dark for the Americans. The country had run out of money, and New Englanders who had opposed the war all along were now talking of *seceding* from the Union. American resistance in the Chesapeake Bay failed, and the British marched into Maryland. The inexperienced Maryland militiamen panicked and ran, and the British troops

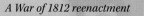

A War of 1812 reenactment

marched on to Washington, D.C., where they set fire to as many government buildings as they could, including the Capitol and the President's mansion.

The British marched next to Baltimore, but the U.S. Army there was able to hold them off. A young lawyer, Francis Scott Key, watched the battle through the long, frightening night and was relieved to see that the American flag still waved above the fort in the Baltimore Harbor the next morning. The British eventually withdrew, and Key was inspired to write the poem that eventually became America's National Anthem: "The Star Spangled Banner."

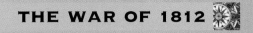

White Paint

When the Madisons returned to Washington after the attack by the British, Dolley said, "We shall rebuild. . . . The enemy cannot frighten a free people." Later, the President's mansion was rebuilt and painted white to cover the scorch marks left on its remaining timbers. It soon came to be called the "White House."

Signing of the Treaty of Ghent

Meanwhile, 10,000 British veterans of the Napoleonic War were advancing on the United States from Montreal. America had no hopes of defeating them on land, and the outcome of the war looked bleak for the United States. But suddenly, everything changed.

On September 11, 1814, American naval captain Thomas MacDonough destroyed the British fleet on Lake Champlain. Fearing loss of communication and supply lines, the British army on land retreated. American peace negotiators across the ocean in the Flemish city of Ghent now had something with which they

*Something that is **ratified** has been formally approved by a governing body.*

could work. The British were tired of war, and they decided to abandon their hopes of gaining territory in North America. For their part, the Americans relinquished their demands that Britain recognize their rights to neutrality. The Treaty of Ghent was signed on December 24, 1814, restoring everything to the way it was before the war. The U.S. Senate unanimously *ratified* the document on February 17, 1815. With a sigh of relief, both sides walked away from fighting. Thousands of lives had been lost, and Britain had accomplished absolutely nothing. On the American side, the war had one very important effect:

Battle of New Orleans

Article of Surrender of Detroit, 1812

American Indians' last real hope of halting the westward rush of white settlers had died.

The war was officially over in December—but word traveled slowly in those days, and the news had not yet reached General Andrew Jackson, who had been busy all this time defending against the British assault to the South.

A small British fleet with three hundred soldiers had entered the mouth of the Apalachicola River in Florida. They built a fort and called on the surrounding Native tribes to join them in their invasion of the Southern states. General Jackson wrote to the U.S. Secretary of War:

> The hostile Creeks have taken refuge in Florida. They are there fed, clothed, and protected. The British have armed a large force with munitions of war, and are fortifying and stirring up the savages. If you will permit me to raise a few hundred militia, which can easily be done, I will unite them with such a force of regulars as can easily be collected, and will make a descent on Pensacola, and will reduce it. I promise you I will bring the war in the South to a speedy termination; and English influence with the savages, in this quarter, shall be forever destroyed.

Florida was Spanish territory, and President Madison didn't want to provoke a war with Spain, not now when the British had all but destroyed the American economy. With only the vaguest of orders, General Jackson assumed responsibility for the assault. He marched on Pensacola and emerged victorious. Unaware that the war was now officially over, he moved next to defend New Orleans.

His troops consisted of a motley crew of volunteers from Tennessee, Kentucky, and New Orleans. The British forces

The British Navy was a powerful force.

Political cartoon describing British invasion of America's rights on the seas

A Reputation for Military Prowess

Even before the Battle of New Orleans, Andrew Jackson had proven he was not a man to yield to difficulties. His reputation for military prowess had already been earned fighting Indians.

Early in the spring of 1814, he drove 1,200 Creek warriors into their fort at Tohopeka. He surrounded the fort, so that escape was impossible, and then set the fort on fire. Almost every Creek warrior died in the flames, and the tribe's military power was forever destroyed. Those who were left sued for peace—except for a few warriors who fled to Florida and joined the tribes there.

outnumbered them by more than two to one. Against these odds, Jackson managed to pull off the most amazing American victory of the entire war.

Jackson's victory at New Orleans gave Americans back their pride. They forgot the way they had limped through the war, facing defeat after defeat, and instead, they remembered the times they had won against incredible odds. From the Northern states to the Southern, from the East Coast to the Western frontier, Americans felt a new unity with one another.

For many Americans, Andrew Jackson was the figurehead for this new spirit of nationalism. As a new national hero, his reputation swelled. The United States had given up on expanding to the north—but its sights were now firmly fixed on the West. What's more, with Andrew Jackson's fierce aggression as their spearhead, America turned its full attention south—to Florida.

Florida's lush growth

Four
THE HISTORY OF FLORIDA

Long ago, the lush warm land the Europeans would call Florida was home to many Native tribes: the Panzacola, the Apalachicola, the Apalachee, the Timucua, the Calusa, and the Matecumbe. The ancestors of these people had traveled thousand of years earlier (perhaps 12,000 years ago) across the ice bridge from Siberia into Alaska. These first explorers and settlers journeyed across the immense continent and eventually made their way to the southernmost peninsula. There they found a rich, fertile home. They learned to live in close relationship with their natural environment, and they looked on the Earth as their mother.

And then one day, everything changed. Enormous tall ships landed on their shores, bringing white-skinned men dressed in metal. Some tribes welcomed the strangers, but many saw them as a threat to their security and way of life. The Natives resisted, but their battle was hopeless before it had even begun.

The white-skinned men from across the sea had more sophisticated weapons and an advanced technology that seemed like magic to the Natives. The strangers' most powerful weapon, however, turned out to be the invisible creatures they carried with them. Neither side knew of the existence of microbes—but the

The Deadliest Enemy

When the first human beings migrated to North America, thousands of years ago during the last Ice Age, they traveled through the frozen wastes of Siberia and across a land bridge in the Bering Strait to Alaska. The trip was a long and difficult one, and many of the germs causing deadly diseases could not survive the migration. Because so many diseases were no longer present, the people gradually lost their natural abilities to fight off the germs that caused them. Their immunities disappeared through thousands of years of not being needed.

Meanwhile, diseases thrived in Europe, where human beings and farm animals lived in close contact, passing germs back and forth. The germs that caused these diseases traveled on the ships with the European explorers and colonists. They brought the most devastating of all changes to Native American civilization.

The Natives had no protection against diseases like smallpox, measles, chicken pox, and malaria—to mention only a few. Sickness spread through the native populations of the New World like an out-of-control forest fire. Within a hundred years of Christopher Columbus's discovery of land on the other side of the Atlantic, approximately 90 percent of Native Americans had died, most of them from diseases unintentionally brought by explorers. Many of the Indians who died had never even seen a white person.

The decimation of the Native American population was a terrible tragedy. European explorers had no idea that simply by making contact with the inhabitants of the Western Hemisphere they were introducing germs that would wipe out entire populations.

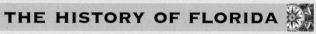

Many Native people died because of the Spanish.

47

Fort Caroline today

microscopic organisms the new people carried would wipe out entire tribes of Native people.

In 1513, nearly a hundred years before the first English would settle Jamestown, Virginia, a Spaniard named Ponce de León set out from Puerto Rico (where he had been the Spanish governor) looking for an island with miraculous waters; he had heard rumors of a fountain of youth, which would make people live forever. When he landed at Eastertime on a green and flowery land, he mistook the peninsula for his magical island. He named it *La Florida*, "The Flowery Place."

By 1565, the Spanish city of St. Augustine had been built, fifty-five years before the Pilgrims came ashore in Massachusetts far to the north. For years, the Spanish considered St. Augustine to be North America's capital city. Their colony endured for more than two hundred years.

France also tried to build a colony in Florida. In 1564, an expedition of three hundred men and women established a settlement named

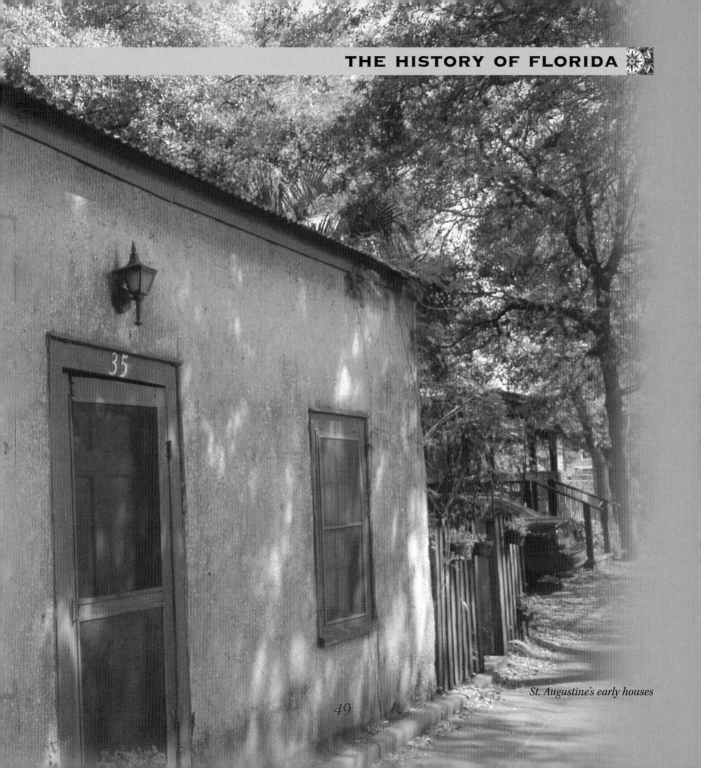

St. Augustine's early houses

49

A cannon at Ft. Caroline

Fort Caroline in northeastern Florida. One of these settlers, a young man, sent this letter home to his father:

> I arrived in this land of New France, prosperous and in good health (thank God), which I pray may be also true of you. I must not fail to take pen in hand and run it over the paper in order to give you a small description of the Isle of Florida, called New France, and of the type and customs of the Natives. . . .
>
> As soon as we were on land we found [a] chief with three of his sons and over two hundred Natives, their women and their little children. The chief was very ancient, and made signs to us saying that he had seen five generations, that is, the children of his children, up to the fifth generation. . . .
>
> I hope to learn to understand the customs of these Natives who are very good people, making trade with them very easy. . . .
>
> I did not want to forget to write you that yesterday, Friday, we captured a big crocodile, like a lizard with arms like a human being with joints, and with five fingers on the front paws and four on the back paws, whose skin was sent to France aboard the ships going back home.

The French had hoped to build a permanent colony in Florida, establishing their presence in North America—but when the Spanish built the city of St. Augustine the following year, they quickly moved to drive out the French. The troops from St. Augustine arrived in the middle of the night, while the inhabitants of Fort Caroline were sleeping. The Spanish swept through the fort, killing the French men, women, and children with their swords and pikes. As many as 143 people were killed in all, and France abandoned the idea of establishing a colony in Florida.

The French flag flying over Fort Caroline

51

After this, Spanish control of Florida remained firm for the next two centuries. The colony never proved to be as profitable for Spain as its colonies in Mexico, Peru, and other regions of the Western Hemisphere, but the Spanish referred to St. Augustine as *la ciudad siempre fiel*—the ever-faithful city.

For the most part, relations between the Spanish newcomers and the Native people were relatively friendly. The Spanish, however, were

convinced that their culture and religion were superior to the Natives', and so **Franciscan** missionaries flocked to Florida, teaching the Natives religion, as well as farming, cattle raising, carpentry, weaving, and reading and writing. By the middle of the 1600s, the Franciscans had built thirty-one missions on the peninsula. In

*A **Franciscan** is a member of the Catholic order of friars and nuns founded by St. Francis of Assisi.*

Florida currency

Autonomous *means independent and self-governing.*

Conquistadors *are Spanish conquerors and explorers, especially those who came to the Americas in the 16ᵗʰ century.*

many ways, these missions were a success; they helped teach the Native people about European culture without trying to exploit or abuse the Indians; in fact, the missions often served as storehouses for Native oral traditions and history.

Spanish society in the fifteenth, sixteenth, and seventeenth centuries was by no means perfect, but it looked on slavery somewhat differently from its English counterparts. Both Africans and Natives were bought and sold as slaves—but unlike English slaves, many Spanish slaves earned wages. They could buy their own homes, and eventually, if they could accumulate enough savings, they could purchase their own freedom. This meant that the line between slavery and freedom was not the solid, impenetrable barrier that it was in the English colonies, and later in the Southern United States.

The Spanish in Florida also allowed the Natives as a whole to continue to live their lives in a fairly *autonomous* society, which the Spaniards called the "Republic of Indians." Unlike the Spanish *conquistadors* in Mexico and Peru, the Florida settlers did not

A Report to Spain

When Bishop Calderón from Cuba visited the Florida missions, he wrote in his report back to Spain that the Natives were "clever and quick to copy any art they see done, and great carpenters as is evidenced in the construction of their wooden churches which are large and painstakingly wrought."

Monument honoring St. Augustine's missionaries

A reconstruction of the interior of a Native home

usually demand that the Native people pay them taxes, nor did they expect them as a group to serve them with backbreaking labor. The Spanish governor of Florida referred to the Natives as "my sons and cousins," an affectionate term of respect. Unfortunately, however, the Native Floridians were a dying population.

Historians today estimate that somewhere between 100,000 and 500,000 Native Americans were living in Florida when the Spanish first arrived in Florida. By 1600, about 75 percent of these people had died, most from disease. When the English built the city of Charleston in 1670, the Carolinas became the center of the Native American slave trade. The Spanish could not prevent English raiders from enslaving most of Florida's remaining 10,000 to 12,000 Natives.

With so few people living in Florida, Spain worried about the economy. No people meant no one to buy and sell things; it also meant no labor force. The Spanish government decided to attract settlers to Florida by recruiting slaves and American Indians living in the English colonies. In 1693, the King of Spain, Charles II, issued a proclamation, promising freedom to any English slave who came to Spanish territory. He was, he declared, "giving liberty to all . . . the men as well as the women . . . so that by

Reconstruction of a Native home

their example and by my liberality others will do the same." In exchange for their freedom, the former slaves would become Catholics and offer Spain military service.

Hundreds of African Americans fled to St. Augustine's Castillo de San Marcos and to another fort in western Florida called Mose. Many of the fugitives built free villages in the wilder-

The French and Indian War, 1754–1763

Indians paying tribute to the French in Florida

Also called the "Seven Years War," this conflict between Britain and its colonies and the French, Indians, Austrians, and Spanish was possibly the first world war. Battles to establish empires were fought across Europe and spilled over to the North American continent. Native Americans fought on both sides, but primarily alongside French troops.

The war ended with the Treaty of Paris, signed in February 1763. France lost all its territory in North America except for some Caribbean islands. Britain received Canada, and Spain received Louisiana to make up for losing Florida to the British.

One of the most important outcomes of the war for America was the planting of the seeds that would lead to the American Revolution. Now that the French were gone from its shores, America no longer needed the British government to protect the colonies from the French. Resentment began to grow among the colonists about the taxes the "mother country" levied on them. The stage was set for the War for Independence.

ness. At the same time, Indian tribes from Georgia and Alabama, especially the Creek, began moving into Florida's lands. These people came to be known as "Seminole," from the Spanish word *cimarrone*, which means "wild, runaway." The term *maroon* came from the same word and was used to identify runaway slaves. The two groups intermarried, and by the 1800s, around 450 Black Seminoles lived in Florida settlements. The Red Seminole had thirty-four settlements by this time, where they farmed and raised cattle and horses.

The Castillo of San Marcos in St. Augustine

England did not appreciate the fact that Spain had no respect for its colonies' "property." In the first years of the eighteenth century, the English governor of South Carolina sent raiding party after raiding party down into Florida. As a result, the Spanish missions came to a sudden and violent end. Most were burned to the ground; many missionaries and Natives were slaughtered; and other Natives were taken captive and sold into slavery. The onslaught of English forces brought tragic changes to Florida.

Most of Spain's power in the Western Hemisphere lay to the south and west, while

*Residents of the American colonies who supported Britain during the Revolution were called **Tories**.*

An ancient clay jar used to collect rainwater under the eaves of Spanish homes in Florida

France and England vied for power in the northern and eastern portions of North America. When the tension between the two countries grew into the French and Indian War in 1754, Spain eventually made the mistake of throwing in its lot with France. In response, England seized the Spanish port of Havana in Cuba.

In the peace treaty that concluded the war, Spain sacrificed Florida in order to get back Cuba. (Things went even worse for France, who gave up all its North American territories—including Canada—to England.) After more than two centuries, Florida was now English.

The new territory was so large that the English divided it into two colonies: East Florida, with the capital at St. Augustine, and West Florida, with the capital at Pensacola. The entire Spanish population in East Florida—3,046 people—immediately took ships to Cuba. Unfortunately, the Native and African inhabitants could not leave so easily. Many of the free people of Florida now found themselves facing slavery.

A few years later, when the other thirteen English colonies revolted against their mother country, the fourteenth and fifteenth colonies (of which history books tend to say very little) remained loyal to the English crown. These colonies became a refuge for *Tories* during the Revolutionary War. Meanwhile, Spain once more sided against the British; this time, it was on the Americans' side.

By the end of the war, Spain had recaptured West Florida, and the treaty that ended the war returned East Florida to Spain as well.

After only two decades, Florida was once more in Spanish hands.

But Florida was all too conscious that the infant United States was growing up. The African and Native residents of Florida were not eager for their home to become part of the "land of the free" (as Francis Scott Key described the United States in the poem he wrote during the War of 1812). Both groups knew if Spain were forced to relinquish Florida to the United States, their lives and liberty would be threatened.

And when General Andrew Jackson turned his fierce eye toward Florida, both Africans and Indians were prepared for a fight.

A rusted cannon from the days when Spain ruled Florida

Five
ANDREW JACKSON'S BATTLE FOR FLORIDA

Spain hoped to control Americans' ***expansionist*** tendencies through trade and immigration. The Spanish government gave special privileges to English companies and Indian traders, in the hopes that the resulting financial prosperity would encourage these powerful Floridians to resist the United States' pressure—and it offered land grants to any settlers who wanted to immigrate to Florida.

This last policy proved to be Spanish Florida's undoing. Instead of encouraging its residents to be less attracted to the United States, it actually accomplished the exact opposite. As more and more American settlers poured into the territory, the percentage of Spanish inhabitants grew less and less. As a result, a large part of the population favored becoming part of the United States.

*An **expansionist** favors the increase in size of a country's economy or territory.*

Museum displays of Seminole warriors

In 1791, U.S. Secretary of State Thomas Jefferson wrote to President Washington:

> I wish 10,000 of our inhabitants would accept the invitation. It would be the means of delivering to us peaceably what must otherwise cost us a war. In the meantime, we may complain of the seduction of our inhabitants just enough to make the Spanish believe it is a very wise policy for them.

In 1810, the residents of Baton Rouge established their own government and declared themselves the "Republic of West Florida." President James Madison took advantage of the event by annexing the land between the Mississippi and Pearl rivers. (Florida at that point extended all the way west to the Mississippi River.)

Many Americans wanted Florida to become a U.S. territory. In 1811, Congress secretly authorized President James Madison to send troops to Florida. During the next three years, the U.S. Army, the Georgia militia, and Tennessee volunteers attacked Spanish and Seminole communities in northern Florida. Seminole warriors fought the American invaders, fiercely defending their land and liberty.

The Black Seminoles were said to fight with the greatest courage, since they were the ones who faced the greatest danger. American

Reconstruction of a Florida settler's home

Brigadier General Thomas Flourney had ordered, "Every Negro found in arms will be put to death without mercy." He told his troops to enslave all blacks they captured. The fighting resulted in few battle-related deaths among the Seminole, but the destruction of cattle and crops caused starvation among the desperate people of Florida.

In the War of 1812, the British threw their lot into Florida's tensions and sided with the Natives, in the hope of driving back the American forces. Thanks to Andrew Jackson's efforts, however (already discussed in chapter 3), the American government was able to annex yet another chunk of Florida, leaving only East Florida under Spanish rule.

Shortly after the War of 1812 came to an end, General Andrew Jackson complained about a "Negro Fort erected during our late war with Britain . . . now occupied by upwards of 250 Negroes, many of whom have been enticed away from the service of their masters."

He was describing Fort Gadsden, located on the Apalachicola River.

The fort's eighteen-foot thick walls and many

Andrew Jackson

Seminoles hid in Florida's many swamps to escape Jackson's troops.

American militiaman

cannons and muskets protected 320 African refugees, both free blacks and runaway slaves. At Jackson's urging, a U.S. gunboat fired a heated cannonball over its wall. The cannonball landed in the ammunition dump and set off an enormous explosion that killed 270 people. The survivors were captured and sold into slavery.

According to Jackson, the Spanish were too weak to control their territory. As a result, the Natives and Africans of Florida were a danger to the United States. If Spain could not govern its lands, then the United States would do the job for them. Jackson's reasoning justified his ***preemptive*** attack on Spanish Florida with a force of 1,800 men (mostly Georgia militiamen and Tennessee volun-

*Something that is **preemptive** is done to stop something else from occurring.*

*A **yardarm** is the end of a long pole that supports the head of a square sail.*

*The President's **cabinet** is a group of advisers, each concentrating on a specific area, such as defense.*

*To **censure** someone is to issue an official expression of condemnation or disapproval.*

Jackson at Pensacola

teers). General William McIntosh persuaded 1,600 Creek Indians to join the fight. They marched through northwest Florida, burning Red and Black Seminole towns.

On April 7, 1818, Jackson arrested and tried two British agents he encountered in Florida, accusing them of arming and inciting the Natives to rise up against the United States. Jackson found the British agents guilty, and one was hanged from the *yardarm* of a U.S. vessel and the other shot. General Jackson then proceeded to Pensacola.

On May 24, 1818, Jackson's troops were outside Pensacola preparing to lay siege to the town. The Spanish governor fled to

Santa Rosa Island and escaped capture. Later, Jackson would say that this was the only great failure of his campaign, his inability to capture, try, and hang the Spanish governor for assisting America's enemies. He made the best of the situation, however, and seized the Spanish capital, declaring himself the new leader of the area until "the transaction can be amicably adjusted by the two governments."

President Monroe was left to clean up the mess Jackson had created. Acting almost completely on his own authority, Jackson had executed two British citizens, seized Spanish land and citizens, and installed American government on Spanish territory. Monroe's **cabinet** recommended that he deny any knowledge of the attack and **censure** or remove Jackson from his position in the U.S. Army.

The American public, however, disagreed. Americans still considered Jackson to be a national hero. His latest campaign only increased his stature in their eyes. Public opinion saved Jackson from disgrace.

But Jackson was shocked and dismayed when the President restored Florida to the Spanish. Heavy campaigning from Jackson and his allies led the House to vote down resolutions supporting the Monroe administration's actions. By this time, however, Spain had realized how easily the United States could take Spain's land for free, and the Spanish government jumped at the chance to sell Florida for five million dollars. Under the terms of Adams-Onís Treaty, Spain ceded Florida to the United States in 1821. Meanwhile, the British, while upset at the killing of two of their citizens, did not wish to enter yet another battle with the United States when the War of 1812 had just been resolved.

Jackson embarked on a victory tour of the United States. The President yielded to public pressure and offered Jackson the governorship of the Florida territory; Jackson resigned from the army to take the new post. On July 17, 1821, Jackson presided over the formal transfer of Florida to the United States, watching as the American flag was unfurled over the former Spanish capital.

Spain had done what it could to protect the citizens it left behind. Article VI of the Adams-Onís Treaty guaranteed freedom to Africans. "The inhabitants of the territories which his Catholic Majesty cedes to the United States shall be . . . admitted to the enjoyment of all

Andrew Jackson and His Wife

Andrew Jackson loved his wife Rachel fiercely. When she was seventeen years old, Rachel Donelson had married Lewis Robards. Robards turned out to be unreasonably jealous, accusing Rachel of unfaithfulness with several men and making her life miserable. In 1790, the Kentucky legislature told Robards he could divorce his wife, since he believed she had been unfaithful to him. Rachel moved out, believing she was now divorced. In 1791, she married Andrew Jackson.

In 1793, Robards finally got around to divorcing Rachel, using the fact that she was living with Jackson as grounds for the divorce. Andrew and Rachel were horrified; their marriage had not been legal since Rachel had not been divorced after all. In 1794, they married again to make it official.

The scandal of his marriage and "adultery" continued to haunt Jackson during his political career. He was intensely protective of Rachel, allowing no one to insult her. This, combined with Jackson's fiery temper, led to a number of duels in her honor.

In 1806, Charles Dickinson made a comment about Rachel, and Jackson called him out for a duel. Jackson was determined to kill Dickinson, even "if he had shot me through the brain." Dickinson shot first, hitting Jackson in the chest. Ignoring the pain (those with him did not even realize he had been shot until much later), Jackson coolly aimed his pistol at Dickinson and fired, killing him. Dickinson's bullet remained lodged in Jackson's chest, causing him pain for the rest of his life.

Rachel died only months before Jackson's inauguration as President in 1829. Bitterly, Jackson blamed those who had harassed her throughout the campaign by slandering her character.

Rachel Jackson

71

*Something that is **nullified** has been made legally invalid, cancelled out.*

Seminoles who fled to Southern Florida

privileges, rights, and immunities of citizens of the United States." The Seminole viewed this provision with hope, believing their Florida residency would give them the protection of U.S. citizenship. Two hundred Black Seminoles knew better than to trust the treaty's terms, and they fled to Andros Island in the Bahamas.

Their fears proved to be accurate. Andrew Jackson's first decree as governor **nullified** Article VI of the Adams-Onís Treaty. All Seminole, black, and mixed-race Floridians were denied citizenship. Jackson also considered the 7,000 Seminole living in Florida to be a major hindrance to its development. The ensuing conflict, known later as the First Seminole Indian War, forced the Indians to move further south to elude capture or death.

Jackson's time as governor was short-lived, however, as he frequently quarreled with the remaining representatives of the Spanish government. Citizens of the area criticized Jackson for his dictatorial manner. Jackson set up a strong governmental structure before he began to think about leaving Florida in late August. His wife's health was suffering in Florida's swamplands, and Jackson also worried that he was being left out of decisions and job postings in Washington. He returned home in November and formally resigned as Florida governor on December 1, 1821.

Conditions in Florida improved little for the Seminole and Africans, however. Slave catchers swarmed into the area, capturing free blacks and Indians, as well as runaway slaves. Life became dangerous and desperate for many people, including those who had once been wealthy and successful citizens.

Zephaniah Kingsley, for example, was the owner of a large and successful plantation, but his wife, Anna Madgigine Jai, was from Senegal, West Africa, and had started life as a slave. She

A Twenty-Year Commitment

When Jackson resigned as governor of Florida, President Monroe appointed William DuVal as governor. On September 6, 1823, DuVal met with seventy Seminole near St. Augustine. They accepted the Treaty of Moultrie Creek, giving up 28 million acres in north central Florida. In return, they received a twenty-year commitment by the United States to respect their four million-acre reservation. The U.S. Army promised peace to the Seminole if they would turn over all blacks living among them. The Seminole refused.

The Kingsley Plantation

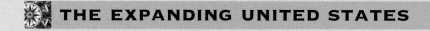

Andrew Jackson is memorialized on the twenty-dollar bill.

76

actively participated in plantation management, acquiring her own land and slaves when Kingsley freed her in 1811. But when Florida became a U.S. territory, the Kingsleys and their four children were no longer accepted in upper-class society. More and more American slaveholders moved into the territory; nervous that African Americans might rebel, the government passed oppressive laws. Conditions for Florida's African population, whether free or enslaved, deteriorated still further. Kingsley was against the restrictive laws, arguing that more humane treatment would create a more stable and peaceful system, but he had little sway over the new American residents of Florida. Eventually, Kingsley and his family fled to Haiti.

Many other African Americans also escaped to either Haiti or Cuba; others fled into the wilderness, along with the Seminole. Life in Florida would never be the same.

Andrew Jackson remained a hero in the eyes of the American public, and in 1829, he became President.

Under his leadership, the U.S. government passed the Indian Removal Act of 1830, which required the 60,000-plus Native people living east of the Mississippi to move west of the river. Some Seminole in Florida complied with the act, but others retreated deep into the Everglades. The Treaty of Payne's Landing required that all Seminole move out of Florida by May 1835, and the U.S. Army arrived to enforce the treaty. This led to the Second Seminole War, fought by some three or four thousand Seminole guerrilla warriors against 200,000 American troops. U.S. forces destroyed Seminole villages and burned their crops. Threatened with starvation, the Seminole finally stopped fighting, although a peace treaty was not signed until 1934. The U.S. government had spent about $20,000,000 on the war, which at the time was an astronomical sum. In the end, the government left the remaining Seminole in peace.

Florida officially became a state in 1845.

Bruin become MEDIATOR or Negociation for PEACE.

Political cartoon symbolizing America's growing power and Britain's diminishing strength

Six

THE UNITED STATES GROWS UP

America was born out of a war of liberation against the world's greatest empire at that time. As a result, its leaders were distrustful of empires. The United States was intended to be an entirely new sort of nation, one built on principles of freedom and equality. These ideals were vital to the way Americans viewed themselves.

But as America grew, these ideals came into conflict with others. On the one hand, the United States wanted equal footing with other nations around the world. This meant that the young country needed a strong army, economic security, and enough territory to ensure that other nations would respect it. Could America expand its boundaries—becoming in effect a new empire—and still maintain its democratic principles?

President Thomas Jefferson had maintained that it could. He used the phrase "empire of liberty" to express his hopes that as America gained more territory, its government would bring the privileges of democracy to its new lands. Future American presidents—like James Monroe—would struggle with the issue, while other Americans, like Andrew Jackson, would feel confident of America's right to expand.

Expansion requires strong armies, however—and armies generally require heavy taxes, which in turn generate large bureaucracies and a powerful centralized government. Many Americans were not comfortable with the

Empires

An empire exists when a government has control over lands that are separate from it, lands that once existed as independent states. One of the earliest and most powerful empires, the Roman Empire, once spread across most of Europe. Centuries later, the great European powers—Spain, England, and France—built their own empires as they colonized the "new land" they discovered in the Western Hemisphere.

When an empire absorbs a smaller and weaker country, it often brings real benefits to that country. Inevitably, however, the gains are balanced by losses that are just as real. According to historian Paul Schroeder, "Those who speak of an American empire bringing freedom and democracy to the world are talking of dry rain and snowy blackness. In principle and by definition, empire is the negation of political freedom, liberation, and self-determination."

United States' growth in these areas. They felt that America should continue to be a nation where ordinary people had the power to govern themselves. Born in the freedom of the American wilderness, they felt their nation should be radically different from old European powers. Representative John Randolph of Virginia expressed these sentiments when he cried: "What! Shall this great mammoth of the American forest leave his native element and plunge into the water in a mad contest with the shark?"

After the War of 1812 and Jackson's invasion of Florida, many Americans worried about the contradiction between America's finest values and its new willingness to use force in pursuit of national interests. On the practical level, many individuals were eager for the opportunities

The concept of the wilderness was important to early Americans' identity.

The Accusations

Andrew Jackson was wounded and infuriated by Henry Clay's accusations. Jackson believed deeply in the Constitution and democratic government, and he did not see that his actions contradicted these in any way. Clay's implication that he was a potential tyrant enraged him even more. "The hypocracy & baseness of Clay," Jackson told a friend, ". . . make me despise the Villain."

they could find settling the new lands that had originally belonged to Native Americans—but other Americans mourned the destruction of Native society. These citizens were not sure that boundless, unrestrained growth was a good thing for the United States.

In the weeks after Andrew Jackson's invasion of Florida, many Americans condemned his hotheaded and aggressive behavior. Thomas Jefferson had once referred to Jackson as a "dangerous man," and politician Henry Clay warned the House of Representatives that military heroes such as Alexander the Great, Caesar, Napoleon—and Andrew Jackson—jeopardized the standards of democracy.

Some Americans, especially *evangelical* Christians, organized mass protests and condemned the Indians' removal from their

Evangelical means relating to any Protestant Christian church whose members believe in the authority of the Bible and salvation through personal acceptance of Jesus Christ.

Native Americans had depended on the land for their way of life.

America's wide-open spaces

*If an organization is **interdenominational**, it is made up of people from different religious groups.*

***Sovereign** means self-governing.*

lands, labeling it a crime against humanity. Jeremiah Evarts, the chief administrator of the American Board of Commissions for Foreign Missions, an ***interdenominational*** missionary organization, exposed and denounced the U.S. attack on Indian sovereignty based on morality, history, and the Constitution. Throughout the colonial period and under the Articles of Confederation and Constitution, Evarts pointed out, various authorities had by treaty guaranteed the territorial integrity of Indian lands. The Native tribes, he insisted, had "a perfect right to the continued and undisturbed possession of these lands." The Indians, he added, were ***sovereign***, as "separate communities, or nations." Removing the Indians from their homes was, in the minds of Evarts and many other critics of aggressive expansion, "an instance of gross and cruel oppression."

Eventually, in the twentieth century, the American government would come to see things from Evarts' perspective, and Indian nations would be treated as sovereign entities. But in the early nineteenth century, voices speaking against expansion were not loud enough to drown out the demands for new land.

In the years that followed the War of 1812, U.S. leaders would begin to use the term "Manifest Destiny" to express America's mission. In other words, Americans believed it was their God-given destiny to acquire new land. Advocates of this ideology believed that the United States had both the right and the obligation to assume control over less-developed areas in the name of democracy, Christianity, and white supremacy.

Things That Build Nationalism in the United States

national heroes
the National Anthem
the Pledge of Allegiance
national holidays that commemorate the country's history

Manifest Destiny justified Americans' settlement of new lands.

As America gained a sense of itself as a nation, it needed to put into words its concept of its own destiny. Americans considered themselves to be hardworking, courageous, and enterprising; their world was boundless, and there were no limits on what American individuals, society, and the nation itself could achieve. This sense of limitless opportunity became linked with a matching belief in geographical limitlessness. America was the place of wide-open spaces—and these spaces should not be restricted by narrow boundaries.

The people of the United States came to believe that their mission was to extend the "boundaries of freedom" to others by imparting their belief in democratic institutions to those who were capable of self-government.

(Unfortunately, Native Americans and other groups of non-European origin were often perceived as being incapable of self-government and so needing additional help from Americans.) These ideas became permanently linked with Americans' concept of their nation's destiny.

In the years that followed, the United States continued to struggle with these same concepts. How do the demands of democracy and human rights balance with the demands of a nation's self-interest? How should these concerns be lived out in practical ways? These issues have been evident throughout America's history of conflict and conquest—and they still play a major role in shaping America.

1803 Thomas Jefferson authorizes the Louisiana Purchase.

1565 Spanish city of St. Augustine, Florida, is established.

1801 Thomas Jefferson is the first President inaugurated in Washington, D.C.

1754 French and Indian War begins.

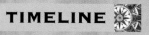

June 19, 1812 The United States goes to war with Great Britain in the War of 1812.

1811 Troops under William Henry Harrison destroy the Shawnee camp on the Tippecanoe River, earning Harrison the nickname "Old Tippecanoe."

August 19, 1812 The U.S.S. *Constitution*, "Old Ironsides," defeats the H.M.S. *Guerriere*.

1810 Residents of Baton Rouge, Louisiana, establish their own government as the Republic of West Florida.

1811 President James Madison sends troops to Florida.

August 1812 General William Hull surrenders the city of Detroit as a result of a failed attempt to invade Canada.

January 8, 1815 Andrew Jackson and his troops defeat the British at the Battle of New Orleans.

August 1814 British troops burn Washington, D.C.

December 24, 1814 The Treaty of Ghent is signed, ending the War of 1812.

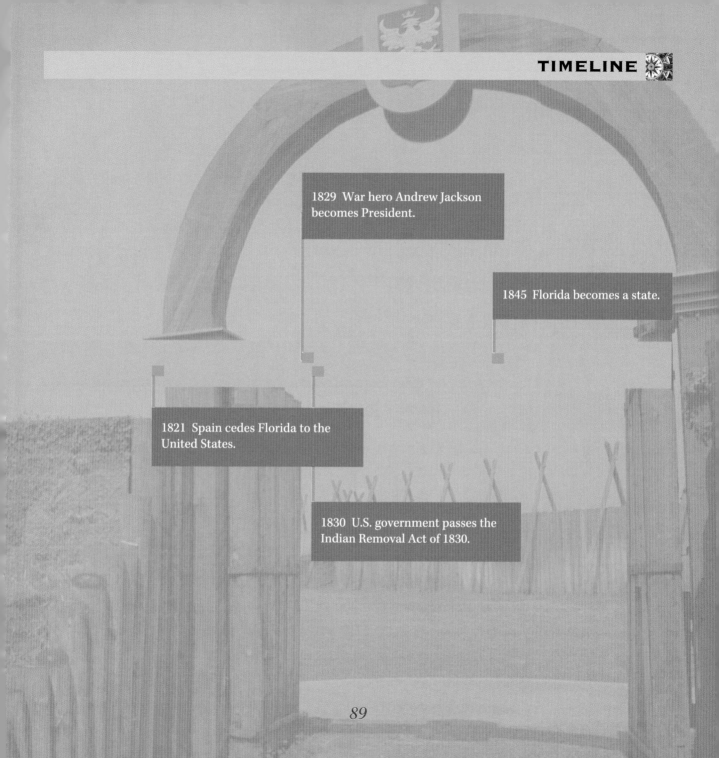

1829 War hero Andrew Jackson becomes President.

1845 Florida becomes a state.

1821 Spain cedes Florida to the United States.

1830 U.S. government passes the Indian Removal Act of 1830.

FURTHER READING

Behrman, Carol H. *Andrew Jackson*. Minneapolis, Minn.: Lerner Publishing Group, 2003.

Borneman, Walter R. *1812: The War That Forged a Nation*. New York: HarperCollins, 2004.

Gannon, Michael. *Florida: A Short History*. Gainesville: University of Florida Press, 2003.

Gillmer, Thomas C. *Old Ironsides*. New York: McGraw Hill, 1997.

Hakim, Joy. *The New Nation 1789–1850*. New York: Oxford University Press, 2003.

Landers, Jane. *Black Society in Spanish Florida*. Chicago: University of Illinois Press, 1999.

Libal, Joyce. *Seminole*. Philadelphia, Pa.: Mason Crest Publishers, 2004.

Martin, Tyrone G. *Most Fortunate Ship: A Narrative History of Old Ironsides*. Annapolis, Md.: Naval Institute Press, 2003.

Stefoff, Rebecca. *Tecumseh and the Shawnee Confederacy*. New York: Facts On File, Inc., 1998.

FOR MORE INFORMATION

Andrew Jackson
www.synaptic.bc.ca/ejournal/Jackson.htm
www.u-s-history.com/pages/h154.html

Old Ironsides
www.ussconstitution.navy.mil

Seminole Wars
plaza.ufl.edu/moverton/html/1stSemWar.htm
www.georgiaencyclopedia.org/nge/Article.jsp?
path=/HistoryArchaeology/AntebellumEra/
Events-7&id=h-842

Shawnee history
www.tolatsga.org/shaw.html

Tecumseh
www.ohiohistorycentral.org/ohc/history/
h-indian/people/Tecumseh.shtml

War of 1812
www.multied.com/1812/Index.html
warof1812.casebook.org

INDEX

THE EXPANDING UNITED STATES

BIOGRAPHIES

AUTHOR

Ellyn Sanna has had a lifelong interest in American history. She is the author of numerous fiction and nonfiction books for both adults and young adults, and she spent several years teaching history to middle-school students. As she researched this book, she traveled to many of the sites involved, giving her a deeper understanding of America's unfolding history.

SERIES CONSULTANT

Dr. Jack N. Rakove is a professor of history and American studies at Stanford University, where he is director of American studies. The winner of the 1997 Pulitzer Prize in history, Dr. Rakove is the author of *The Unfinished Election of 2000, Constitutional Culture and Democratic Rule,* and *James Madison and the Creation of the American Republic.* He is also the president of the Society for the History of the Early American Republic.

PICTURE CREDITS

Albert Bierstadt: p. 85

Asher Brown Durand: p. 84

Benjamin Stewart: pp. 1, 44, 48–50, 55–57, 57, 59, 60–63, 64 (right and left), 65, 67, 96

Canadian Library and Archives: p. 16

Currier & Ives: p. 15

Department of the Army: pp. 23 (right), 38–39,

Fort Caroline National Memorial, National Park Service, Photographer Benjamin Stewart: pp. 48, 51, 74–75, 88–89

Frederic Edwin Church: p. 81

George Catlin: pp. 82–83

Library of Congress: pp. 25 (right), 42, 44–45, 47

National Archives and Records Administration: pp. 37, 42–43, 86–87

Photos.com: pp. 41, 72–73, 76, 81

University of Texas: p. 35

U.S. Navy: p. 29

Valley Forge Convention and Visitor Bureau: pp. 36–37